Life in the New American Nation™

The Federalists and Anti-Federalists

How and Why Political Parties Were Formed in Young America

Gregory Payan

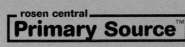
rosen central
Primary Source™
The Rosen Publishing Group Inc., New York

For Kate Giese, Greenville's prettiest Anti-Federalist

Published in 2004 by The Rosen Publishing Group, Inc.
29 East 21st Street, New York, NY 10010

First Edition

Library of Congress Cataloging-in-Publication Data

Payan, Gregory.
The federalists and anti-federalists: how and why political parties were formed in
young America / by Gregory Payan.— 1st ed.
     p. cm. — (Life in the new American nation)
Includes bibliographical references and index.
Contents: Building the United States government—Two opposing political parties—After ratification of the Constitution—The beginnings of the "new" Republican Party—Political parties today.
ISBN 0-8239-4038-1 (lib. bdg.)
ISBN 0-8239-4256-2 (pbk. bdg.)
6-pack ISBN 0-8239-4269-4
1. Political parties—United States—History—Juvenile literature. [1. Political parties—History.]
I. Title. II. Series.
JK2260 .P39 2003
324.2732'09'033—dc21

                                                                          2002152851

Manufactured in the United States of America

Cover (left): Portrait of James Madison

Cover (right): The Republican National Convention

Photo credits: Cover photos (left and right), pp. 1, 7, 12, 15, 22, 25 © Library of Congress; pp. 10, 11 © *The American Revolution: A Picture Source Book*, Dover Pictorial Archive Series; pp. 19, 27 © Hulton/Archive/Getty Images; p. 20 © National Archives and Records Administration.

Designer and Photo Researcher: Nelson Sá; Editor: Eliza Berkowitz

Contents

Introduction

In 1776, the people living in the thirteen colonies decided to become independent from England. They had been protesting against British rule for years. They decided it was time to fight for their freedom.

After five years and many battles, the United States won their independence. The next step was to set up a national government. A group of very different state governments had to come together and form a union. They wanted it to be powerful but in no way to resemble a tyranny. A tyranny is a government that is cruel or unfair to its citizens. The British ruled their colonies under a tyranny. The new, free United States would not rule in the same way. The new U.S. government would represent its citizens in a fair way. The majority of the people's views would be represented. The United States would never ignore the views of the minority.

The Articles of Confederation was written in 1777. It explained how the American government would be set up. The Articles of Confederation held the states together during the war with England. However, a new, more complete document was needed. The United States needed something that would govern the union for a long time. Americans were uncertain about the form of their new government. They wanted it to be strong, but they didn't want to take away the power of the state governments that were already in place. It was a very hard task for the young nation.

In May 1787, fifty-five representatives from all the states arrived at the Constitutional Convention. They met to try and create the perfect government. The representatives elected George Washington as president. He was a Revolutionary War hero. He had the support and respect of the other representatives. Washington knew it would be hard to get the states to believe in the union. Washington and his fellow representatives wanted to make the U S. government successful.

Chapter 1

Two Opposing Political Parties

Over the next three and a half months, the U.S. Constitution was written. There was a great deal of arguing among the representatives. Eventually, however, they agreed the document was finished. The Constitution was sent to all of the states for approval. Nine of the thirteen states needed to approve the Constitution for it to be ratified, or approved. Once ratified, it would become the model for the government of the United States. During this process, the American people would see the power of political parties for the first time.

Two political parties that had been around for years would now become well known. They were called the Federalists and the Anti-Federalists.

This is a photograph of the original U.S. Constitution. The original document is housed in Washington, D.C., at the U.S. National Archives and Records Administration (NARA) building. The Constitution helped young America form its own government. Many different opinions and views had to be taken into account for the Constitution to be ratified.

The Federalists were in favor of ratifying the Constitution. The Anti-Federalists were against it. They now decided to take their arguments to the citizens of the United States. Through speeches, booklets, and newspaper articles, each party hoped to convince the people that its view on government was the best one.

The Federalist Party was founded in 1787. The Federalists were largely made up of wealthy people from the North. They favored a strong central government and a national bank. The party's early leaders were Alexander Hamilton, John Jay, James Madison, and George Washington.

The Anti-Federalists were mostly from the South. They favored strong state governments and individual rights. Most of their supporters owned a lot of land. Many owned slaves. They felt the Anti-Federalists best represented their political views. Samuel Adams, George Mason, and Patrick Henry led the Anti-Federalists.

Even before America won its independence, the Federalists and the Anti-Federalists had argued at the Constitutional Convention. They fought about religion, land, and British rule. Once the United States needed to create its own government, the two parties fought more than ever. It was a very important time in the nation's history. Both parties had ideas on how best to create a strong union. Both also felt that their ideas were the best for the future of the country. The decisions being made would affect the United States for hundreds of years. Each side wanted their views to be reflected in the Constitution.

A Famous Speech

Before the American Revolution, Patrick Henry made one of the most famous speeches in U.S. history. While speaking to the colonists of Virginia at a church in Richmond, he encouraged the colonists to get weapons and fight the British. He said, "Is life so dear or peace so sweet, as to be purchased at the price of chains and slavery? . . . I know not what course others may take; but as for me, give me liberty or give me death!"

The Federalists felt the Constitution as it was written would be better for them and their supporters. The Anti-Federalists did not feel the Constitution would benefit them. They hoped that the states would not ratify it.

The Anti-Federalists faced a difficult challenge. It would be hard to prevent the Constitution from being ratified. By letting the people know their views, they hoped that public support would force the government to make changes. The changes they wanted would guarantee the rights of state governments and the rights of United States citizens. The Federalists, on the other hand, only needed to make sure the Constitution was ratified. This would be best for their party and their supporters. Both parties communicated with the public through the Federalist and Anti-Federalist Papers.

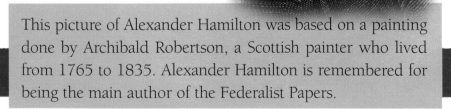

This picture of Alexander Hamilton was based on a painting done by Archibald Robertson, a Scottish painter who lived from 1765 to 1835. Alexander Hamilton is remembered for being the main author of the Federalist Papers.

Alexander Hamilton was the main author of the Federalist Papers. Hamilton was a brilliant writer from New York who had a background in law. He was in favor of a strong central government. He believed in the Constitution. Hamilton felt that New Yorkers needed to be convinced that the Constitution should be ratified. By handing out the Federalist Papers, he hoped to sway their opinions. The Federalist Papers were published in newspapers in New York four times a week during 1787 and 1788 under the anonymous name "Publius." Hamilton, along with John Jay

This picture of James Madison was published in *Leslie's Magazine* 100 years after the Constitutional Convention. Madison, a Federalist and America's fourth president, helped Alexander Hamilton write the Federalist Papers.

and James Madison, published eighty-five essays. Each paper told the people why they should support the Constitution. They also argued that what the Anti-Federalists were saying was wrong. The Federalist Papers were eventually collected and published as a book.

The Anti-Federalists hoped to accomplish the opposite of what the Federalists were doing. They warned people about the Federalists. They told the people that they should fear a strong central government. Samuel Adams and Patrick Henry wrote most of the Anti-Federalist Papers. The Anti-Federalists

This portrait of George Mason was created by Albert Rosenthal in 1888. Mason was a famous Anti-Federalist. He was a member of the Constitutional Convention and believed strongly that slavery was wrong and should not be legal.

claimed the Constitution would cause the government to become too powerful. They claimed it would make the president like a king, it would favor the rich over the poor, big states would be favored over small states, and no individual rights would be given to the citizens.

One at a time, Hamilton and the other Federalists picked apart each of these arguments in the Federalist Papers. They explained why the position of the Anti-Federalists was wrong. Both parties published many papers, but in the end the Federalists won the support of the public.

On June 21, 1788, New Hampshire became the ninth state to ratify the Constitution. Important votes in New York and Virginia had not happened yet, but it wouldn't matter. When New Hampshire ratified the Constitution, it became the law of the land.

Chapter 2

After the Ratification of the Constitution

In the early 1790s, Democratic societies and Republican clubs began to form. These were smaller political parties. They hoped to challenge the power of the Federalists. Eventually, the two groups came together. They formed the Democratic-Republican Party. They were led by Thomas Jefferson and James Madison. Madison had originally been an important member of the Federalist Party. He was even one of the authors of the Federalist Papers. Madison left the Federalists to support Jefferson and his views.

The Democratic-Republicans took the place of the Anti-Federalist Party. Jefferson felt that the government should protect a person's rights to life, liberty, and happiness. He believed that the greatest danger to that freedom was a tyrannical government. Much like the Anti-Federalists, Jefferson thought states should have the most power because they were less likely to misuse it. Many people rallied behind Jefferson. He was a great believer in liberty and had drafted the Declaration of Independence in 1776. The Federalists were beginning to lose power and public support.

George Washington led the Federalists. They worked to improve the nation. Alexander Hamilton was named secretary of the Treasury. A national bank was created under their rule. The Federalists settled the problems of debt left

This is a portrait of Thomas Jefferson, the third president of the United States. He is most often remembered for drafting the Declaration of Independence. He was also a strong supporter of the Anti-Federalist Party.

Dueling for Revenge

Alexander Hamilton was involved in one of the most famous duels in history. A duel is an organized fight between two people using weapons. In 1804, Aaron Burr, an important member of the Federalist Party, ran for governor of New York. Hamilton encouraged voters not to vote for Burr, and Burr lost. Burr was furious and challenged Hamilton to a duel. On July 11, 1804, Burr shot Hamilton in the stomach, and Hamilton died the next day.

over from the Revolutionary War. They also improved the country's relationship with England.

In 1798, the Federalist government passed the Alien and Sedition Acts. These acts caused James Madison, one of their most powerful members, to leave the party. It was also the beginning of their loss of the people's support. The Alien Act made it more difficult for an immigrant to become a United States citizen. It allowed for the detention of immigrants during wartime and also allowed the president to deport, or force to leave the country, anybody he chose. The Sedition Act outlawed public criticism of the government in power.

Jefferson and Madison feared that the government was becoming too powerful. Jefferson and Madison responded by passing the Kentucky and Virginia

Resolutions. The resolutions said that states did not have to obey Congress if the laws they passed exceeded Constitutional authority.

Thomas Jefferson became the third president of the United States in 1801. At the time, he was running as a Democratic-Republican. The Democratic-Republican Party won every election from 1800 to 1824. In 1828, "Republican" was dropped from the party name, and Andrew Jackson, a wealthy slave owner, became the first Democratic representative for president.

From 1801 to 1815, the Federalists tried to rally support against the Democratic-Republican administration. They had little success. They had many candidates, but most were unsuccessful in elections. By 1824, the Federalists were no longer an important force in politics. It would be many years before the wealthy citizens of the United States had a party that would support them and challenge the power of the Democrats.

Chapter 3

The Beginnings of the Republican Party

Andrew Jackson was voted into the presidency in 1828. This meant that the Democrats were firmly in power. They had won seven presidential elections in a row. Their political views were widely accepted in American society. These views mostly favored the working class. However, wealthy Americans were determined to gain more power. Many parties that opposed the Democrats began to grow in the 1830s and 1840s. These parties were mostly made up of wealthy merchants and abolitionists. Abolitionists were against slavery. The Democrats and most of their supporters were in favor of slavery. Slaves worked on the huge plantations, or farms, that were important

This image of slaves being transported was made by Eyre Crowe in the 1850s. One difference between the major political parties was how they felt about slavery. The Democrats at that time were in favor of it, while the political parties that opposed them were not.

to the U.S. economy. The nation had relied on this business for over a hundred years.

The Whig Party was one of the political groups that had beliefs different from those of the Democrats. The Whigs began to gain power from 1834 to 1836, mostly in the North. They were made up of people who did not like President Andrew Jackson. During this time, Jackson was securing his second term as president. Jackson had upset a lot of people by pushing for small farmers and workers to have a voice in government. The Whigs would challenge the Democrats and gain power. William Harrison, John Tyler, Zachary Taylor, and Millard Fillmore all served as president under the party banner in the 1840s and 1850s.

This is a copy of a lithograph made in 1848 by James Bailie. It shows the Battle of Molino del Rey, one of the battles in the Mexican-American War. The Mexican-American War lasted for three years, and the United States won battle after battle.

In 1848, another new party was organized. It was called the Free Soil Party. Members of this party opposed the spreading of slavery into territories acquired by the United States after the Mexican-American War. The United States had battled Mexico for three years in the 1840s and gained more territory. While many people had thought that the United States shouldn't be fighting Mexico, the Mexican-American War helped the westward expansion of the United States. After the war, the United States's territory included present-day Texas, New Mexico, Arizona, and California.

Kansas and Nebraska were established as United States territories in 1854, and they applied for statehood. The Democratic government, led by President Franklin Pierce, responded by repealing the Missouri

Who Were the Know-Nothings?

The Know-Nothings were a political party made up of Irish and German immigrants. Their official name was the American Party. Their interesting name didn't mean they were not smart. They wanted to keep their members and political views secret. Party leaders told members that if they were ever questioned about the party, they were to say they "know nothing" about it.

Compromise. This upset many citizens. The Missouri Compromise, passed in 1820, said that there would be no slavery in states above a certain latitude. The Democratic government repealed it, however, so that the new states, Nebraska and Kansas, could determine for themselves if they wanted slavery. The more state

An oil painting by George P. A. Healy of President Abraham Lincoln meeting with military advisors in City Point, Virginia, in February of 1865. From left to right: William T. Sherman, Ulysses S. Grant, Abraham Lincoln, and David S. Porter.

governments and citizens that wanted slavery, the more support the Democrats received.

Most of the new political parties that were against the Democrats began to strongly resist slavery in the new states. Since many of these parties had similar views against the Democrats, it also made them come together. In this way, they could challenge the power of the Democrats. Nearly all abolitionists, along with the Whigs and the Know-Nothings, came to join the Republican Party. The Republican Party now had enough members to be an effective voice in government. In 1861, Abraham Lincoln became the first Republican elected as president. He would lead the United States in the most difficult time in its history: the Civil War. From the 1850s through today, the Democratic and Republican Parties remain the two most powerful parties in the United States government.

Chapter 4   Political Parties Today

In the beginning of our nation's history, it was difficult for people to form and accept political parties. People formed groups based on the property they owned. They formed parties to represent their interests in government. At first, opposing parties would attack their enemies with the hope of destroying them. In the 1780s, political parties were made up of people who had different jobs, rather than different views about politics. The views of the farmers often opposed the views of merchants and shippers. As time went on, political parties hoped to gain support from the people. They also wanted to defeat their opponents in government.

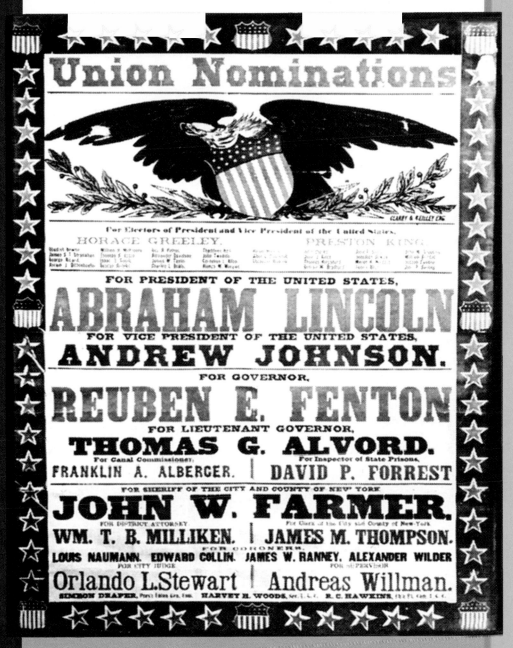

This is a poster from Abraham Lincoln's second presidential campaign in 1864. Lincoln won the election but did not live to complete his second term. On April 14, 1865, Lincoln was shot by John Wilkes Booth, a supporter of slavery. Lincoln was the first president to be assassinated.

25

In the past, if the people of a country had different views than those of the ruling group, they might want to overthrow the government and remove it from power. Often, it involved many people being killed. In the United States, people were beginning to feel that they could hold different views and still be loyal to the same government. Once the Federalists and Anti-Federalists began to accept each other's beliefs, it was easier for the groups to compromise. While holding different views, they both believed that the United States of America could be strong. This belief produced the acceptance of two parties in the eyes of the American public.

Other parties have come and gone since the Civil War. The Democrats and Republicans, however, have had the most impact in elections. Many smaller political parties exist today, but no parties have the influence or public acceptance of the Democrats and Republicans. They have the longest history, the most members, and the most money.

Political parties are needed to identify candidates and to help them gain support among the people. If

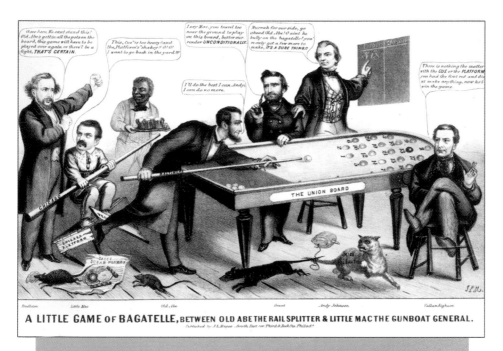

A LITTLE GAME OF BAGATELLE, BETWEEN OLD ABE THE RAIL SPLITTER & LITTLE MAC THE GUNBOAT GENERAL.

This is a political cartoon from the 1864 presidential race. Abraham Lincoln (depicted making a shot during a game of pool) won the election over Democrat George B. McClellan, pictured holding a cue stick behind Lincoln.

a party is successful and its candidate is elected, the hope is that the candidate will govern and express the views of his or her supporters. The system is not perfect, but it tries to uphold its ideals. It features representation for all people and supports a federal union of states under one federal government. The government protects the citizens of the United States and also protects itself.

Glossary

anonymous (a-NAH-nih-mus) Written by a
person who hides or does not give his or
her name.

colony (KAH-luh-nee) A place that is controlled by
a governing body that is far away.

compromise (KOM-pruh-myz) Something midway
between two things; a promise in which each side
gives up some demands.

debt (DET) Something that is owed to another.

deport (dih-PORT) To banish someone from
a country.

detention (dih-TEN-shun) To keep in custody;
confinement.

encourage (in-KUR-ij) To help or to give support to
a person or idea.

exceed (ek-SEED) To go beyond a limit.

expansion (ek-SPAN-shun) The enlargement or
increase in size of a piece of land or territory.

future (FYU-chur) That which will happen in time; an occurrence that will happen later in time.

government (GUH-vern-mint) An organization that governs and rules a city, state, or body of people.

guarantee (gar-an-TEE) An assurance that there will be a certain outcome; a promise that a product is in good condition.

immigrant (IH-muh-grint) A person who comes to a new country to live.

latitude (LA-tih-tood) The position of a place, measured in degrees north or south of the equator.

liberty (LIH-ber-tee) Freedom from control of someone or something more powerful.

ratify (RA-tih-fy) To approve.

representative (reh-prih-ZEN-tuh-tiv) A person authorized, usually by an election, to speak on behalf of others.

sedition (sih-DIH-shun) The stirring up of rebellion against the government in power.

tyranny (TEER-uh-nee) An unjust government.

unite (yoo-NYT) To bring together so as to make one in common interest or cause.

Web Sites

Due to the changing nature of Internet links, the Rosen Publishing Group, Inc., has developed an online list of Web sites related to the subject of this book. This site is updated regularly. Please use this link to access the list:

http://www.rosenlinks.com/lnan/feaf

Primary Source Image List

Page 1: Watercolor on paper of the west front of the United States Capitol. Painted by John Rubens Smith in 1830.

Page 7: The document "The Constitution of the United States of America" established the government of the United States. It is housed in the National Archives and Records Administration (NARA).

Page 10: Engraving of Alexander Hamilton by Archibald Robertson. Created in 1790.

Page 11: Engraving of James Madison by H. B. Hall Jr., from the original by G. Stuart. Published by *Leslie's Magazine*.

Page 12: Painting of George Mason, created by Albert Rosenthal in 1888.

Page 15: Portrait of Thomas Jefferson. Engraving after painting by Rembrandt Peale in 1790. Housed in the University of Chicago Library, American Historical Portraits, William E. Barton Collection of Lincolniana.

Page 20: Lithograph of the Battle of Molino del Rey by James Bailie in 1848. Housed in the National Archives and Records Administration (NARA).

Page 22: Oil painting by George P. A. Healy in 1865.

Page 25: Lincoln campaign poster from 1864. Housed in the Library of Congress.

Page 27: Illustration published by J. L. Magee in 1864.

Index

About the Author

Gregory Payan is a freelance author who resides in Forest Hills, NY, with his wife, Casey.